Welcome to Australia

By Mary Berendes

The Child's World®

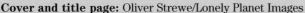

Published by The Child's World®
1980 Lookout Drive
Mankato, MN 56003-1705
800-599-READ
www.childsworld.com

Content Adviser: Jeff Collman, Ph.D., Associate Professor,
Georgetown University, Washington, DC
Design and Production: The Creative Spark, San Juan Capistrano, CA
Editorial: Publisher's Diner, Wendy Mead, Greenwich, CT
Photo Research: Deborah Goodsite, Califon, NJ

Cover and title page: Oliver Strewe/Lonely Planet Images
Interior photos: Alamy: 18 (Hemis), 20 (Simon Grosset), 23 (Bill Bachman); Corbis: 3, 9 top
(L. Clarke), 17 (Jose Fuste Raga); 3, 19 (Stephanie Maze); iStockphoto.com: 28 (Ufuk Zivana), 29
(Tamara Murray), 30 (Susan Stewart), 31 (Anne Clark); Landov: 16 (Sophie Hares/Reuters), 25
(David Davies/EMPICS); Minden Pictures: 7 (Mark Moffett); NASA Earth Observatory: 4 (Reto
Stockli); Photolibrary.Com (Australia): 6 (Peter Walton), 8 (Wu Norbert), 9 bottom (Doug Perrine),
10 (Jacob Halaska), 14 (Frances Andrijich), 15 (Trevor Worden), 21 (Robin Smith), 24 (Peter
Harrison), 3, 27 (David Messent); Photo Researchers, Inc.: 13 (William D. Bachman).
Map: XNR Productions: 5

Library of Congress Cataloging-in-Publication Data
Berendes, Mary.
  Welcome to Australia / by Mary Berendes.
    p. cm. — (Welcome to the world)
  Includes index.
  ISBN-13: 978-1-59296-910-4 (library bound : alk. paper)
  ISBN-10: 1-59296-910-0 (library bound : alk. paper)
  1. Australia—Juvenile literature. I. Title.

DU96.B475 2007
994—dc22
                                   2007005551

Contents

Where Is Australia?

From high above, Earth looks like a big, blue ball. But if you look closely, you can see many things. The blue patches are really oceans and seas. There are also huge brown and green patches. These are land areas called **continents.** Australia is a continent. It lies between the Indian Ocean and the South Pacific Ocean.

Some of the world's continents are made up of many countries. But Australia is different. Only one country can be found there—Australia.

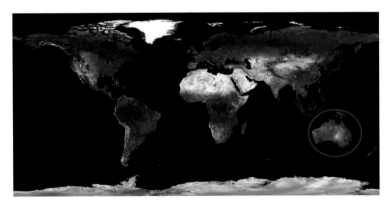

This picture provides a flat view of Earth. Australia can be found inside the red circle.

Did you know?

Australia is the sixth largest country in the world. It also includes Tasmania, an island off the southeastern coast.

4

INDONESIA

PAPUA NEW GUINEA

AUSTRALIA

⊛ National capital

★ Other capital

• Other city

EAST TIMOR

Arafura Sea

Timor Sea

★ Darwin

Gulf of Carpentaria

Great Barrier Reef

Coral Sea

INDIAN OCEAN

Northern Territory

Queensland

Western Australia

South Australia

★ Brisbane

New South Wales

Perth ★

Great Australian Bight

★ Adelaide

Sydney ★

Canberra ⊛

Australian Capital Territory

Victoria

★ Melbourne

N

W E

S

Bass Strait

Tasman Sea

0   200   400 miles

0   200   400 kilometers

Tasmania

Hobart ★

INDIAN OCEAN

The Land

Most of Australia is low, flat, and dry. Many areas are covered with short bushes and grasses. In some places, there is nothing but sandy desert. There are also low mountains and flat areas called **plateaus.** A plateau is an area of land that is higher than the lands around it. Some of Australia's plateaus have rich soil that is good for farming. Other plateaus are covered with grass and forests.

A vineyard in Hunter Valley

Nambung National Park near Perth

Did you **know?**

The equator is an imaginary line that goes around Earth.
Countries that lie above the equator have seasons at the same
time as the United States. But Australia lies below the equator.
It has its seasons at the opposite time. So when it's winter in
the United States, it's summertime in Australia!

Plants and Animals

Kangaroos can only be found in Australia.

Australia is known for its strange and beautiful creatures, such as **marsupials.** Marsupials carry their young in pouches. Kangaroos, koalas, and wombats are all Australian marsupials. Australia is also home to the dingo, a kind of wild dog. Many beautiful birds, such as parrots and lyrebirds, live there as well.

English settlers brought new animals into the country. Before they arrived, there weren't any sheep or cattle living there. The settlers also introduced Australia to other kinds of dogs and birds, too.

Two important kinds of plants in Australia are the eucalyptus (yoo-kuh-LIP-tuss) and the acacia (uh-KAY-shuh).

Koalas like to eat eucalyptus leaves.

Acacia plants are often found in dry areas. Eucalyptus trees grow in wetter places. Many kinds of wildflowers also grow in Australia.

Did you know?

Just off the northeastern coast of Australia lies the Great Barrier Reef. It's a chain of more than 2,500 coral reefs. Many plants, fish, and ocean animals depend on the reefs for food and shelter.

A group of aborigines who live in the Northern Territory

Long Ago

The **Aborigines** (ab-uh-RIJ-uh-neez) were the first people to live in Australia. They probably came to the continent from South or Southeast Asia. The Aborigines traveled in groups from place to place. They have hunted and lived on Australia's lands for more than forty thousand years.

The first visitors to Australia were traders known as the Macassans. In 1770, Captain James Cook first saw Australia. He claimed the land for Great Britain. Great Britain first used part of the country as a place to hold prisoners. Later, other settlers moved to Australia to start new lives. Great Britain ruled Australia for many years.

Did you know?

Australia is really called "The Commonwealth of Australia."
People just say "Australia" for short.

Australia Today

Since 1906, Australia has had its own government. It has its own flag and its own national song. But Australia still has many ties with Great Britain. Australians speak English just as the British people do. And the queen of Great Britain is still very important to many Australians.

Aboriginal people still live in Australia, too. The British took away land from the Aborigines when they settled there. But in recent years, laws have been passed to return some areas of the country to the Aborigines. Aboriginal leaders are working with the government of Australia to improve their people's lives. They have created special programs to help the Aborigines become healthier, get better schooling, and find better jobs.

Some people have moved to Australia from other countries. After World War II, many Europeans, especially those from

Aboriginal children have a reading lesson.

Greece, settled in Australia. In recent years, people from many Asian countries have moved there, too. In fact, people from around the world now make Australia their home.

People enjoy a holiday near Perth.

The People

Australia has lots of beaches.

About 20 million people live in Australia. Most of them live along the eastern and southeastern coasts. They like to live there because the central parts of the country are too dry and hot.

Many Australians are **descendants** of the British settlers. Many others are **immigrants,** or newcomers from other countries. Aborigines still make up a small part of the population, too. Australians are very friendly people. They welcome new faces and love to smile. They also like to have fun!

City Life and Country Life

Almost all of Australia's people live in cities. These cities have shops, restaurants, and tall buildings just like those in the United States. But apartment buildings are very rare in Australia. That's because most people live in small houses called **bungalows.**

Australians call the countryside "the bush" or "the outback." Only a few people live there. To get around, people must use small planes. That's because there are very few smooth roads in the outback. By flying planes, people can check on farm animals, look at crops, and even go to town for groceries!

In the outback, some people use planes to travel from place to place.

16

The Sydney Opera House (left) is one of the city's most famous buildings.

Schools and Language

Australian children start school when they are about five years old. They learn math, reading, science, and writing just as you do. But in the outback, students live too far away to attend regular schools. Instead, they learn through correspondence schools and schools of the air.

This child learns at home through schools of the air.

In correspondence schools, students receive and turn in their homework by mail. In schools of the air, teachers and students talk to each other on two-way radios and other devices.

English is the main language in Australia. It was brought over by the British settlers. Australians also use Aboriginal words to describe things. "Koala" and "kangaroo" are both Aboriginal words.

Two students in Melbourne

A cattle ranch in West Australia

Work

Australians have all sorts of different jobs. Some people work in offices or in factories making paper or clothes. Others fish for lobsters, oysters, and shrimp. Still others work in the forests cutting lumber for building.

A farmer looks after his wheat crop.

The best-known job in Australia is farming. The wide, open spaces of Australia's countryside are the perfect place for raising such animals as cattle and sheep. The wool and meat from these animals can be sold to people all over the world. Many other Australian farmers raise apples, sugarcane, and wheat. These, too, are sold all over the world.

Food

Australians eat many of the same foods we do. Meat, potatoes, and bread are all favorite items. Fresh vegetables and fruit are popular, too. Just like in the United States, Australians like foods from other countries. Italian, Greek, and Chinese dishes are all popular in Australia.

Did you know?

Many Australians enjoy eating a spread called Vegemite. It tastes very salty and a bit bitter. They put Vegemite on bread or crackers and often have it with their breakfast.

Many Australians like to go boating.

Pastimes

Rugby is a popular sport in Australia.

In Australia, people like to do many things. Some people like to watch television or visit with friends. Most Australians like to do things outdoors. Surfing, swimming, tennis, golf, and boating are all favorite pastimes in Australia.

Team sports are also very popular. Rugby is one team sport that is very rough and dangerous. Players push and shove each other to get at a ball. Another sport many Australians like to play is football. It is similar to American football but uses some different rules.

Did you know?

One famous song in Australia is called "Waltzing Matilda." But it's not about a girl who is dancing. The song is really a story about a wanderer. He carries all of his belongings in a kind of bag called a swag.

Holidays

Australians celebrate many of the same holidays we do. They also have special days of their own. One special holiday is Australia Day. It is celebrated every year on January 26. On this day, Australians remember when the first British settlers arrived in their country. With its fireworks and flags, Australia Day is a lot like the Fourth of July in the United States.

Anzac Day is another important day for many Australians. Every April 25, the country remembers a sad moment in Australian history. The day honors Australian soldiers who died in World War I at the Battle of Gallipoli. It is a bit like Veterans' Day in the United States.

Australia is known for its wide-open spaces, its bright sunshine, its strange animals, and its happy people. Perhaps one day you will visit this wonderful land. If you do, be ready for a good time—Australia is sure to make you smile!

Fireworks are often a part of Australia Day celebrations.

Fast Facts About Australia

Area: About 2,967,920 square miles (7,686,880 square kilometers)—a little smaller than the United States.

Population: More than 20 million people.

Capital City: Canberra.

Other Important Cities: Sydney, Melbourne, Brisbane, Perth, Adelaide.

Money: The Australian dollar. An Australian dollar is divided into 100 cents.

National Holiday: Australia Day, January 26.

National Language: English.

National Flag: Blue with the flag of Great Britain in the upper left corner. There are also a lot of stars on the flag. The biggest star stands for Australia. The smaller stars represent the Southern Cross, a group of stars in the sky.

Head of Government: The prime minister.

Head of State: Queen Elizabeth II of Great Britain.

Famous People:

Edmund Barton: Australia's first prime minister

Sir Howard Florey: Nobel Prize-winning scientist

Catherine Freeman: Olympic athlete, runner

Evonne Goolagong Cawley: famous athlete, tennis player

John Howard: politician, prime minister

Steve Irwin: naturalist, preservationist, television host

Eddie Mabo: lands rights advocate

Narritjin Maymuru: artist

Nellie Melba: Famous opera singer

Roma Mitchell: famous lawyer, judge, and politician

National Song: "Advance Australia Fair." A special song is also played for Queen Elizabeth II of Great Britain. It is called "God Save the Queen."

"Advance Australia Fair"

Australians all let us rejoice,
For we are young and free;
We've golden soil and wealth for toil;
Our home is girt by sea;
Our land abounds in Nature's gifts
Of beauty rich and rare;
In hist'ry's page, let ev'ry stage
Advance Australia Fair.
In joyful strains then let us sing
Advance Australia Fair.

Beneath our radiant Southern Cross
We'll toil with hearts and hands;
To make this Commonwealth of ours
Renowned of all the lands;
For those who've come across the seas
We've boundless plains to share;
With courage let us all combine
To Advance Australia Fair.
In joyful strains then let us sing
Advance Australia Fair.

Australian Recipe:

Damper is a traditional type of Australian bread that is often made using a campfire. It's easy to make and tasty to eat.

2 1/2 cups self-rising flour
1 teaspoon salt
1 teaspoon butter
1 teaspoon sugar
1 cup milk

Have an adult help you preheat the oven to 350 degrees Fahrenheit. Mix the flour, salt, sugar, and butter in a large bowl. Add the milk to the mixture. Stir the ingredients until the dough is well mixed. Then take a round cake pan or a baking sheet and lightly coat it with a little bit of butter and flour. Take the dough out of the bowl and make into a circle shape. Place the dough in the pan. Let an adult put it in the oven and bake for 30 minutes. Once it's done, the damper is ready to eat. Try it with some jam, butter, or honey.

How Do You Say...

ENGLISH	AUSTRALIAN	HOW TO SAY IT
hello	g'day	guh-DAY
friend	mate	MAYT
What?	Ay?	EYE
Oh my!	Blimey!	BLY-mee
No problem	No worries	NO WUR-eez
thank you	ta	TAH
See you later!	Hooroo!	HOO-roo
Australia	Oz	AWZ

Glossary

Aborigines (ab-uh-RIJ-uh-neez)
Aborigines were the first people to live in Australia.

bungalows (BUNG-uh-lohz) A bungalow is a small house with one floor. Many Australian city-dwellers live in bungalows.

continents (KON-tih-nents) Earth's huge land areas are called continents. Australia is a continent.

descendants (di-SEND-uhnts) People who come from a common ancestor, or relative, are called descendants. Many Australians are descendants of early British settlers.

immigrants (IM-ih-grents) Immigrants are newcomers from other countries. Many Australians are immigrants.

marsupials (mar-SOO-pee-yullz)
Marsupials are animals that carry their young in pouches. Kangaroos, koalas, and wombats are all marsupials.

outback (OWT-bak) The outback is the empty, central area of Australia. Not many people live in the outback.

plateaus (pla-TOHZ) Plateaus are flat areas that are higher than the land around them. There are many plateaus in Australia.

Further Information

Read It

Prosser, Robert. *Australia.* New York: Facts on File, 2004.

Sayre, April Pulley. *G'day, Australia.* Brookfield, CT: Millbrook Press, 2003.

Steele, Philip. *Sydney.* Milwaukee: World Almanac Library, 2004.

Look It Up

Visit our Web page for lots of links about Australia:
http://www.childsworld.com/links

Note to Parents, Teachers, and Librarians: We routinely verify our Web links to make sure they are safe, active sites—so encourage your readers to check them out!

Index